ADDRESS THE MESS

NORTH POINT
RESOURCES

ADDRESS THE MESS

Study Guide

Here are some ideas to get you started.

LEADERS:

Need some help? It's okay. We all do.

A full walk-through of the study guide with notes on how to navigate each session is available at **groupleaders.org/addressthemess.**

VIDEOS:

The video sessions that complement this study can be found on the:

- **Anthology Mobile App** (free on the Apple App Store and Google Play)
- *Address the Mess* DVD (available on Amazon)

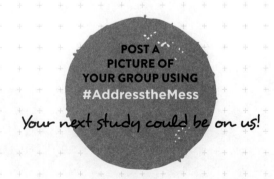

POST A
PICTURE OF
YOUR GROUP USING
#AddresstheMess

Your next study could be on us!

1. HANG OUT.

(about 30 minutes)

Our lives move so fast these days. Take some time to talk about what's going on in the lives of those in your group. Asking about things like job interviews, the health of their kids, and how their weeks are going goes a long way in building community.

2. WATCH THE VIDEO AND DOODLE ALONG.

(about 20 minutes)

When we designed this study guide, we had note-taking in mind. So while you're watching the video, take advantage of the extra space and grid pages for notes and/or drawings, depending on your note-taking style.

3. DISCUSS AND COMPLETE THE ACTIVITIES.

(about 45 minutes)

Depending on the session, your group will have Discussion Questions and scenarios to think through, as well as activities to do. Putting pen to paper can give you deeper insight into the content.

4. PRAY.

(about 5 minutes)

Keep it simple and real. Use the prayer provided. Ask God to help you apply what you've learned that week.

PART 1

The Mess in the Mirror

VIDEO RECAP

Good news. It's not just **you**.

Christians believe:
The mess that brings us _____ is
the mess that brought God _____.
The mess is a **lens** through which we **discover** God.

"But nobody's _____."
There is a **perfect** that nobody **is.**

> *Now we know that whatever the **law** says, it says*
> *to those who are **under the law**, so that **every***
> *mouth may be **silenced** and the whole world held*
> *accountable to God. Therefore no one will be*
> *declared **righteous** in God's sight by the **works***
> *of the **law**; rather, through the law we become*
> ***conscious** of our sin...For **all** have **sinned** and*
> *[all] fall short of the **glory** of God.*
>
> (Romans 3:19–20, 23)

_____ of our messes awakens us to something outside of us to which we are **accountable**.

I know a mess when I **see** one, because I **am** one.

Answer Key for Blanks

together	perfect
near	Awareness

Notes

LET'S TALK ABOUT IT

1 When there's a mess at home or at work, do you tend to jump right into cleanup mode or do you feel overwhelmed? Why do you think you respond the way you do?

2 Why do you think it's so hard to admit when things are a mess?

3 In the message, Andy said, "When it comes to the people around us whose lives are messy, we should be students, not critics."

    A. Write down the name of a person or group of people you find it easy to judge based on their messes.

    _____

    B. Now write down something you can do to be a student rather than a critic (i.e., to learn the story behind their messes).

    _____

    _____

    If you want, share your answers with the group.

4 Have you ever met a person whose messes prevented him or her from believing that God could respond with love? Did his or her belief ever change and if so, how?

5 The harder we work to get a right standing with God, the more aware we become of our shortcomings. Is there a law you're under that's reminding you of a standard you don't meet?

6 Our shortcomings are also reminders of how much we need God. Is this comforting to you? Frustrating? Motivating? Why?

THIS WEEK, THINK ABOUT...

Is there anyone or any group you secretly condemn or judge?

After this week's discussion, can you find common ground with that person or group?

When you find yourself thinking of that person or group, say to yourself, "I know a mess when I see one, because I am one."

PRAYER

God, help me to recognize and acknowledge the messes in my life so they don't stand between you and me. Help me to experience your grace and to know that through Jesus, you don't judge me based on my messes.

I KNOW A *mess* WHEN I SEE ONE *because* I AM ONE.

PART 2

Best Mess Ever

VIDEO RECAP

Your mess has the potential to bring God near to you.

> *For God did not send his Son into the world to _____ the world, but to _____ the world through him.*
>
> (John 3:17)

Jesus told the adulterous woman, "Look at **me**."
Jesus told Zacchaeus, "Come down to **me**."
To the woman at the well married five times, Jesus said, "Come close to **me**."
To the man on the cross, he said, "You're coming **with me**."

Jesus offered **himself** as the **solution**.

> *When Jesus spoke again to the people, he said, "I am the **light** of the world. Whoever **follows me** will never walk in darkness, but will have the **light of life**."*
>
> (John 8:12)

Follow **me**.

*Therefore everyone who **hears** these words of mine and puts them into **practice** is like a wise man who **built** his house on the rock. The rain came down, the streams rose, and the winds blew and beat against that house; yet it did not fall, because it had its **foundation** on the rock.*

(Matthew 7:24–25)

You can't _____ your way out of a

mess you _____ yourself into.

You can **follow** your way out.

I **messed** up. I **gave** up. I **looked** up. God **showed** up.

POST A PICTURE OF YOUR GROUP USING #AddresstheMess

Your next study could be on us!

LET'S TALK ABOUT IT

1 John 3:17 says, *"For God did not send his Son into the world to condemn the world, but to save the world through him."* Does this match your earliest impression of God? Is it how you think of him now?

2 Many people's stories include, "I messed up. I gave up. I looked up. God showed up." Can you describe an experience like this from your life or the life of someone you know?

3 What are some practical ways to follow Jesus when you're in the middle of a mess?

4 In the message, Andy said, "Jesus did not pull back from messy people." Do you know anyone who follows Jesus' example in this way? What would it look like for you to do so?

5 What mess are you dealing with right now (at home, at work, in your finances)? Take a few minutes to individually to write down how you could take the steps that Jesus offered to the messy people he met.

- **"Look at me."**
  How can you recognize Jesus' presence in your life?

- **"Come down to me."**
  How can you move away from your mess and toward Jesus?

- **"Come close to me."**
  How can you draw strength from Jesus?

- **"You're coming with me."**
  What can you do to follow Jesus?

If you feel comfortable doing so, share your responses with the group.

THIS WEEK, THINK ABOUT...

Read back over Matthew 7:24–25 (you can find those verses in the Video Recap).

What's one thing you can do this week to put God's Word into practice in each of these areas of your life?

- Your finances
- Your work
- Your family relationships

PRAYER

God, I messed up. I don't want to give up. My eyes are on you. Please show me the way forward. Show me the way out. I trust you.

THE MESS
that *brings* us
TOGETHER IS WHAT
brings God
NEAR.

PART 3
Inside Out

VIDEO RECAP

Christians believe Jesus _____ the little messes, all the messes of the _____. But, he loves us too much to _____ us that way.

Christianity is not just about staying out of trouble.

> *I thank my God every time I remember you. In all my prayers for all of you, I always pray with joy because of your partnership in the gospel from the first day until now, being confident of this, that he who began a good work in you will carry it on to completion until the day of Christ Jesus.*
>
> (Philippians 1:3–6)

Christianity is an _____ _____ faith.

*And this is my **prayer**: that your **love** may*
abound** more and more in **knowledge** and **depth
*of **insight**, so that you may be able to **discern***
*what is **best** and may be pure and **blameless***
for the day of Christ.

(Philippians 1:9–10)

POST A
PICTURE OF
YOUR GROUP USING
#AddresstheMess

Your next study could be on us!

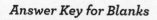

Answer Key for Blanks

loves	leave
world	inside out

LET'S TALK ABOUT IT

1 At some point in your faith, did you assume you had to earn God's approval with good behavior? Where do you think you got that idea?

2 How does the pattern of Christians messing up, seeking forgiveness, and then messing up again influence the way people outside of the faith view the church?

3 Andy suggested that following Jesus is not primarily about trying harder to behave better, but instead about letting God change you on the inside. What do you think about this?

4 In the scenarios below, talk about what it would look like to respond in such a way that your love for other people "may abound more and more."

SCENARIO #1

A colleague publicly takes full credit for a project on which you two collaborated. How do you respond?

Notes

SCENARIO #2

You learn that a friend has repeated something to others that you told him or her in confidence. How do you respond?

SCENARIO #3

A family member asked your advice but did not do what you suggested. Now things aren't going well for him or her. What do you do?

5 Consider the following statements and fill in the blanks.

I'm a better _____ than I was five years ago. In five more years, I want to be a better _____ than I am now.

In light of what you just wrote, why do you think you're better than you were five years ago? Did your behavior change or did your heart change? Or both?

6 Cleaning up a mess takes time. Unfortunately, there's no quick fix that will make you suddenly more happy, healthy, wealthy, or powerful. What are some good things that might happen on the inside—in your heart—as a result of taking the time to work through a mess?

THIS WEEK, THINK ABOUT...

Following Jesus isn't primarily about doing what's right. It's about doing what's right *for others*.

Fill in some of the blanks with things you've prayed for in the last week.

- Help me to _____.
- Help my _____ to _____.
- Keep me from _____.
- Give me _____.
- Bless my _____.

How could you reframe those prayers to instead be about learning and discerning how to best love other people?

PRAYER

God, I don't just want to stay out of trouble. Complete the work you've begun in me—help me see as you see and do as you say. Teach me to love others the way you love me.

YOU **CANNOT** PRAY YOUR WAY OUT OF A *mess* THAT YOU BEHAVED YOUR WAY **INTO,** BUT *you* CAN FOLLOW YOUR **WAY** *out.*

Video Notes

PART 4
Messy–er

VIDEO RECAP

DAVID'S STORY

- When David was a shepherd boy, the prophet Samuel came to his house and anointed him to be king of Israel.
- Problem: Israel already had a king.
- Then there was that David and Goliath thing.
- David becomes an overnight sensation.

"In everything he did he had great _____..."

(1 Samuel 18:14)

- Eventually, Saul does try to kill David.
- David flees.
- Then it seems that the Lord has delivered Saul into David's hands.

Ignore **virtue** and you will eventually make a **mess**.

*Then David went out of the cave and **called**
out to Saul, "My lord the king!" When Saul
looked behind him, David bowed down and
prostrated himself with his face to the ground
… This day you have seen with your own eyes
how the Lord delivered you into my hands in the
cave. Some urged me to **kill you,** but I **spared
you;** I said, 'I will not lay my hand on my lord,
because he is the Lord's anointed.' … May the
_____ judge between you and me.
And may the Lord avenge the wrongs you have
done to me, but **my hand** will not touch you.*

(1 Samuel 24:8, 10, 12)

I'm opting for _____ over

_____ - _____.

Every mess comes **prepackaged** with some
bad options.

POST A
PICTURE OF
YOUR GROUP USING
#AddresstheMess
Your next study could be on us!

Answer Key for Blanks

success	virtue
Lord	hurt-you

LET'S TALK ABOUT IT

1 What is one thing in your life (finances, health, responsibilities) you wish there was a quick fix for?

2 Talk about a time when you faced a mess and either tried or resisted the quick fix. What happened?

3 Andy defined virtue as integrity, honesty, patience, and self-control.

    A. Write down then share your personal definition for one (or more) of those characteristics. Or talk about someone you know who consistently displays one of those qualities.

    B. Place check marks in the two columns below and if you're comfortable, share your responses with the group.

	Which is the hardest for you to exhibit when you're in the midst of a mess?	Which is most likely to land you in a future mess?
Integrity		
Honesty		
Patience		
Self-Control		

4 In the passage Andy presented (1 Samuel 24:1–13), it would have been easy for David to assume that God had purposely delivered Saul into his hands. When you're in the middle of a mess, how do you discern what God is asking you to do versus what your emotions may be convincing you to do?

5 What are some practical ways to identify the virtuous options for fixing a mess?

THIS WEEK, THINK ABOUT...

At the root of most personal messes is a breakdown of virtue (integrity, honesty, patience, and self-control).

Ignore virtue and you will eventually make a mess.

You can't clean up a mess caused by a failure of virtue with another failure of virtue.

Think about a mess you're currently facing.

1. What's the story you want to be able to tell one day?

2. How can you display integrity, honesty, patience, and self-control?

3. Who will hold you accountable for choosing the virtuous solution?

PRAYER

Dear God, when I'm tempted to take the easy way out, help me do the right thing. Give me the courage to be _____ (generous, kind, patient, self-controlled) even when it's difficult. And help me trust you with the outcome.

IGNORE VIRTUE
and you *will*
EVENTUALLY MAKE
a mess.

POST A PICTURE OF YOUR GROUP USING #AddresstheMess

Your next study could be on us!